2nd Stories

A Hoosier photographer explores
what's upstairs, on top, and overhead

Landing (Willard Library), Evansville—Vanderburgh Co. (562-11)

SI STUDIO INDIANA

Photography by John Bower
Text by John & Lynn Bower

Foreword by Michael Atwood

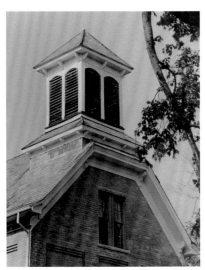

Former school (A Step Back Banquet Hall),
New Washington—Clark Co. (576-03)

Indiana Arts Commission
Connecting People to the Arts

This activity is made possible in part
by the Indiana Arts Commission, a state
agency, with funds from the Indiana
General Assembly and the National
Endowment for the Arts

Published by:

Studio Indiana
430 N. Sewell Road   Bloomington, IN 47408
(812) 332-5073   www.studioindiana.com

©2005, Printed in Canada

Publisher's Cataloging-in-Publication Data
Bower, John.
2nd Stories: A Hoosier photographer explores what's
upstairs, on top, and overhead / text by John Bower and
Lynn Bower; photography by John Bower;
foreword by Michael Atwood.

                              p.   cm.
ISBN-13: 978-0-9745186-2-6
ISBN-10: 0-9745186-2-X
1. Indiana—Description and travel—Views.
2. Architecture—Indiana.
3. Photography, Artistic.
I. Bower, John, 1949–.   II. Title.
TR659.B69   2005
779.944—dc22
Library of Congress Control Number: 2005907076

Foreword

While looking at some of the images you're about to see in John Bower's youngest book, *2nd Stories: A Hoosier photographer explores what's upstairs, on top, and overhead*, I was reminded of a time when I was videotaping rural settings in southern Indiana. The audio guy and I had spent the previous day feasting our eyes, and camera, on a veritable farm dinner-table heaped with rustic barns settled amidst picturesque fields and pastures—enough to satisfy a big, hard-working family, and even the Parson, should he happen by.

But come Breakfast time, early next morning, my visual taste buds were hankering for a scene that was a little different. So we jostled off, along old asphalt back roads, then bounced onto the dusty roar of gravel. The production van rumbled around a few more snaky curves and then—Behold!

Patiently waiting all these years. Growing, changing. Often overlooked and, eventually, forgotten. But now, simply perfect, as the early morning sun crept toward those few brief moments photographers graciously call the "magic hour." A special span of time, when the sun is a most friendly and loving source of illumination.

I gazed in glee at our discovery, and it was a good one, just on the other side of a rusty farm fence that had probably spent the last 20 years in retirement. No farm building was in sight, but we had passed one, maybe a tenth-of-a-mile back. If someone didn't want us around, they'd let us know. We got our gear and headed toward a most scrumptious find.

As we videotaped, on this gorgeous late summer morning, we soon heard the steady putt-putt of a tractor engine drawing near. A moment later, it rounded a curve and rolled into view. The farmer at the wheel looked like he had just steered that tractor right off the cover of Farm Bureau Magazine. He was sporting comfortable blue coveralls, and a cap that proudly proclaimed the superiority of a particular brand of seed. His gaze was aged with furrows of experience.

He didn't mind we were there, but he certainly was puzzled. Why were we so interested in his old forgotten trash heap of abandoned cars and farm machinery?

I tried to explain. The heritage and the metaphor. The goals and the dreams—both real and forgotten—that this big ol' heap of rusting metal symbolized.

He removed his hat and scratched his head—a clear sign of impending prophesy in these parts. A rural sage, he proceeded…

"Seems to me there's just lots purt'yer things to be takin' pictures of. But suit yerselves. Jess be careful." Then he settled back, put the tractor back into gear, and disappeared around the next bend.

I imagine John Bower has had similar experiences in his travels—folks rubbing their chins in contemplation, wondering why this fellow is so interested in this particular fire escape, that particular chimney.

John Bower's newest book continues his love of exploration, paying close attention to the everyday stuff of life— stuff that often escapes attention. In this collection, he encourages all to simply lift their gaze a bit and discover a magnificent world we seldom notice—a place between sky and ground, where we find second stories.

The images in *2nd Stories* reveal a deep curiosity for the otherwise forgotten and overlooked. In these pages, you'll discover another world, one that is still, quite simply, our world. A universe of the intricate and the simple, often residing, virtually ignored, right over our heads, or just out of sight: the dove-white detail of a church steeple, the patient strength of framed timbers in a dusty loft, the doily-carved cornice of a Victorian home.

There is a keen awareness in *2nd Stories* to a common, yet lovely, human experience. Imagine walking down a street, or driving through a city or town, your mind full of appointments, to-do lists, dinner plans, and dreams of winning the Lottery. As you walk, or maybe rest momentarily at a stoplight, your gaze, so briefly, looks up. You are, basically, just staring off into space, as your mind mulls and churns the vast complexities of your life.

You lift your gaze from this river of activities, for just the briefest of breaths. Then it happens. Maybe it's a gargoyle statue peering out from atop the library. Or the way the light is hitting the old water tower just that instant.

Suddenly, you find yourself distracted from the noisy babble, just long enough to actually *see* something—for the very first time! You experience a jeweled moment of new discovery, before the light changes and you must drive away. John Bower has captured this simple, yet revelatory, experience—again and again—in *2nd Stories*.

Places seldom seen, like an attic, have a life beyond our gaze. But we hold an unspoken, yet certain, faith that they'll always be right there, just above us, supporting the roof over our heads—as well as a couple old bowling balls gathering dust, next to the boxes of Christmas decorations. Faith, after all, is a deep belief in the certain reality of the unseen.

John takes us to typically unseen places, with a remarkable faith in their beauty. At first glance, you might think he's only there to observe quietly. But these ordinary observations inspire extraordinary journeys—to hear the stories these spaces tell, paradoxically sharing their rich past even as they affirm their eventual decay.

Other spaces delight in having found a continued, or even a surprisingly new, existence with another generation, their heritage a quiet backdrop to brand new dreams. John's work may capture a singular moment, but in this moment, he tenderly cradles past, present, and future.

2nd Stories also offers the only opportunity many of us will ever have of seeing the normally unseen superstructures of places ranging from county courthouses to downtown businesses. Ever wonder what was in the upper recesses of your local fraternal lodge? Well, you just might find out, in *2nd Stories*.

John Bower reminds us that the rare beauty of everyday life waits just outside the fringes of our attention. Discovering this dimension is as easy as lifting our eyes to a second-story window. A focused attention, on the often overlooked things around us, is both prayer and meditation to John Bower. John invites us to raise our gaze— and pay attention.

Michael Atwood
Host of "Across Indiana"
August 2005

Introduction

I first became intrigued with attics as I a young kid, when my family lived in the small northwest Indiana town of Fowler. It started at Grandpa and Grandma Mendy's house—a small, late-Victorian, frame home. The upstairs was unheated, and consisted of two bedrooms with variously sloped-ceilings, a short hallway, and two irresistible walk-in attic spaces.

Throughout her life, Grandma saved everything under the sun, and stored it neatly away in her attic cubbyholes. Assortments of odds-and-ends—far too precious to throw out—were tucked into shoe boxes, cookie tins, cardboard cartons, old dressers, and mothball-laden wardrobes. The smallest items went into match boxes or aspirin tins. There was an historical archive of postcards, greeting cards, and letters, all organized by year and tied neatly into bundles with string. She also squirreled away outdated military uniforms, decades-old hats, yellowing newspapers (with historic dates), and grade-school projects. In one drawer, I found small boxes of costume jewelry carefully wrapped in tissue paper, glass vials containing tiny sea shells sorted by color, $3^1/_2$ sets of false teeth, and dozens of used pencils (some sharpened down to nubs, but none with teeth marks). In short, those two attics were a veritable museum—an archeologist's or small boy's dream—and I loved exploring them.

Although we moved 30 miles away from Fowler just after I entered first grade, to the (comparatively) large city of Lafayette, I continued visiting those attics well into adulthood. After I married Lynn (also a curious a soul), she readily joined me on trips to Fowler for visits, cutthroat games of Uno, and attic forays. No matter how many times I explored, I always found something that I'd never seen before. Those attics mesmerized me, and they foreshadowed a curiosity about the upper levels of buildings that would endure for decades.

By the time I ended my elementary-school years, Weber's Hobby Shop had become a favorite haunt. It offered everything from plastic model kits, to balsa wood, to finely detailed HO-gauge steam engines. During my model-airplane phase, someone suggested forming a club. The idea probably originated with my friend Tony, who worked part-time at Weber's. After a few people expressed interest, Tony hung a sign-up sheet in a prominent location in the store, and we spread the word to others when out flying our planes on weekends. As enthusiasm grew, Mr. Weber offered his store's second floor as a meeting room, and the Lafayette Cloud Jockeys was born.

All I remember about the club is that most of the members were older guys, and the meetings were tedious and boring. But I still remember Mr. Weber's upstairs. Like many downtown businesses, the hobby shop only occupied the first floor. Although I had been patronizing the place for a few years, I had never considered the fact that there might be anything more to the building than the ground level. But there was—an entire second story, consisting of a single, large, open room with a high, tinned ceiling. It was completely empty except for a few dusty cartons, and the table and chairs we dragged up there for our meetings.

The exterior of the hobby shop had a large display window at street level with a false front above, so the second floor's tall windows couldn't be seen from the outside. From the simple style, I'd guess the façade had been spruced up in the 1950s, perhaps as much as a decade before I discovered it. To get to the upper level, it was necessary to go through a cluttered storage room, then climb the worn treads of a long and creaky stairway, which I recall having surprisingly ornate spindles.

Soon after ascending Mr. Weber's back stairs for the first time, I found myself looking up at other downtown businesses and quickly realized how many had second, third, even fourth stories, and that most were off-limits to the public. As I began eyeing these other buildings, I could see that many upper levels had never been remodeled. Some had fantastic architectural details—cast-iron decorations, carved woodwork, I even saw faces and creatures. On the backs and sides of a few buildings I spotted fading advertising signs promoting cola, bread, and other commodities. The more I looked up, the more I became aware of another world.

As the years drifted by, I had the good fortune to visit the interiors of some of the upper stories I had been noticing. Some were converted to apartments, some were used as warehouses, one was an artists' studio, but many were empty—filled only with shovelfuls of dust and forgotten memories. Yet, no matter what their current use, they still interested me, not only for what they had become, but for what they had once been. I came to realize that, a century or so earlier, when each of these buildings was erected, the *entire* structure was used for something. Perhaps you climbed the stairs to additional sales space, a dance hall, a lawyer's or accountant's office, or an illegal speakeasy. In any case, there was something going on up there. Today, most people have no idea what lurks in the upper levels of old buildings. I'm sure some simply don't care, but I'm just nosey enough to want to explore such spaces whenever possible.

One such opportunity came on a Saturday morning back in the 1970s. when Lynn and I happened to be inside the ornate Tippecanoe County Courthouse. All the county offices were closed for the weekend, yet the building was open, for a reason that now escapes me. We were just wandering around when Lynn spotted an inconspicuous door that was ajar. I pushed it open to reveal a tall set of wooden stairs rising up—to somewhere. There wasn't anyone around to ask permission, so we started climbing—and ended up inside the dome.

To say the least, it was a remarkably special place. The normally hidden support structure of iron plates, beams, and rivets was all exposed and, in the center, a set of spindly cast-iron stairs rose up to the very top, where we could see the mechanism for the dome's clock. Lynn placed her hand on the railing, causing the entire stairway to shake. It was obviously not OSHA-approved, so we decided not to climb any further. But there was still a lot to admire about the magnificence of the place—the sheer volume of the dome, the meticulous craftsmanship, the architectural design. Sadly, this extraordinary space was only being used for storage of old records.

Not long after our courthouse investigation, a fellow I was working for purchased an old 4-story (5 if you counted the basement) brick-and-limestone building a block away from the Courthouse that had most recently belonged to a roofing contractor. After taking possession, we had to deal with decades of accumulation. The place reminded me somewhat of Grandma and Grandpa's attic, but a great deal messier. Amid the piles of trash, there were beat-up office desks and file cabinets, brittle asphalt-shingle samples, window frames with broken panes of glass, and hundreds of rolls of wallpaper that crumbled when unrolled for inspection. It certainly looked as if everything was destined for the dumpster but I kept rummaging through the detritus for treasures.

Just as I was about to give up, I was drawn to a cardboard carton tucked behind a pile of trash. Inside, amid more rubbish, I discovered a pair of odd-looking mechanical devices. As I turned them over in my hands, they increasingly sparked my interest. Each was constructed of two cast-brass pieces which were loosely fastened together and slid in an arc, as well as a pair of concave wooden rollers, one twice the diameter of the other. It took me several minutes to realize what I'd found—the hardware for the top of an antique rolling library ladder. I quickly claimed them and, although it took two decades, I was eventually able to incorporate them into the house Lynn and I built for ourselves.

Over the years, my fondness for the upper levels of buildings—both inside and out—has continued to grow. Without even thinking about it, I look up whenever I enter a new town, or pass a country church, or spot an isolated, railside grain elevator. The eyes of most people tend to look straight ahead, as if they were wearing vertical blinders, so I sometimes feel like a bit of an oddball with my head tilted back. But I occasionally influence others to look up as well—and they usually smile at something they had never noticed—yet had been in plain sight all along.

As Lynn and I were driving around southern Indiana for our last book project (*Guardians of the Soul*), we passed through dozens of Hoosier towns, large and small. In each, we routinely craned our necks to see the upper portions of buildings, pointing out interesting architectural details to each other. At one point, Lynn suggested that these gems deserved a book of their own—and she coined a title: *2nd Stories*. I liked the idea immediately, but wasn't convinced her title was the best choice. After all, we were admiring some third and fourth stories, not just seconds. So we considered alternative titles such as *Heightened Vision*, *A Higher Viewpoint*, and *A Different Perspective*, but none clicked.

The more we deliberated, the more *2nd Stories* sounded right. Then an obvious fact occurred to us. The word "story" didn't just refer to a different level in a building —it also meant a narrative, or an account of something. And with that realization, the title stuck, fitting perfectly a book which, as a photo essay, tells a visual *story*. Plus, for many of the older structures, it is a *second* story—a record of how they appear today, after they've changed and aged over the decades.

So, that's how this project started. Of course, like all major endeavors, the basic concept grew, changed, and matured, as it progressed. For example, it didn't take long before we began noticing all sorts of things up in the air, such as tall, industrial, brick chimneys, bridges, and Eiffel-like microwave towers. As a result, it became important to include captivating structures other than buildings. Originally, I planned to simply shoot the upper levels from atop a step ladder, but once I actually started taking pictures, I realized I'd be using a variety of perspectives. These included close-up details, as well as straight-on shots. Sometimes I'd frame only the upper portion of something, other times I'd capture the whole structure— placing it in the context of its surroundings.

These refinements to my original mission led to the *upstairs, on top, and overhead* of the subtitle. The common denominator is that these subjects can only be seen by elevating your perspective. That is, you need to lift your eyes, or climb, above the *terre firma*, to which gravity, and habit, so firmly adheres us. When looking at these images, you'll begin to realize how much is missed if your visual world is limited to ground level. In fact, I guarantee you'll begin looking up more often, and your world will become larger, more expansive, and dramatically more three-dimensional. Those vertical blinders will be relegated to the past.

John Bower

Building façade, Princeton—Gibson Co. (531-10)

Building detail, New Harmony—Posey Co. (514-11)

Building façades, Petersburg—Pike Co. (532-07)

Building façades, Seymour—Jackson Co. (542-07)

Irwin Gardens, Columbus—Bartholomew Co. (545-14)

13

Sculptural detail, Corydon—Harrison Co. (563-08)

Sculptural detail, Evansville—Vanderburgh Co. (559-15)

Sculptural detail, Jasper—Dubois Co. (551-07)

Sculptural detail, Evansville—Vanderburgh Co. (558-12)

Borden Museum, Borden—Clark Co. (568-04)

(Above) Philanthropist William W. Borden (1823-1906) was a staunch believer in improving rural education. Having a deep interest in geology, he was able to amass a fortune from gold mining, using it to establish an Institute, Library, and Museum in his hometown of New Providence (later renamed Borden in his honor). The Borden Museum's vast collection included his geological specimens as well as pioneer tools and books. It was acknowledged to be one of country's best. Today, the building is used as a community center.

Building detail, Columbus—Bartholomew Co. (470-06)

Building detail, Bloomfield—Greene Co. (534-04)

Building detail, New Albany—Floyd Co. (569-04)

Building detail, Scottsburg—Scott Co. (576-04)

Margaret Mary Community Hospital, Batesville—Ripley Co. (501-06)

Rivet Middle/High School, Vincennes—Knox Co. (527-10)

Merom Conference Center

"Is that for real?" we said in unison, as the sight of a huge, brick, 19th-century building loomed above the trees ahead of us. John and I were driving south on State Road 63 toward the small town of Merom. It was late afternoon, and all day we had seen attractive, but typical, southern Indiana scenes—rolling fields, patches of woods, and disappearing small towns—but whatever was up ahead was totally unexpected. Without hesitation, John drove straight to the grounds of a 5-story marvel. At the entrance we read a sign explaining that this was the Merom Conference Center, which was part of the United Church of Christ. But it began as the Union Christian College in 1859—just before the Civil War—and had remained so until 1924. Today, it serves as a retreat, a summer camp, and a facility for gatherings and meetings.

Near the huge main structure, we could see smaller, newer buildings scattered around. As we approached, a smiling woman told John that he could only shoot pictures from the road, as there was no one around with the authority to allow us onto the campus. It was understandable, as there were dozens of young campers wandering about.

A few weeks later, arrangements were made, and we were back. We met Dale Dressler, the Director, and volunteer art teacher Fred Robberts, who would both accompany us into the main building—College Hall. In communicating with Dale by email, John had learned that the attic might yield the best pictures, so that's where we were headed. As always, it was a pleasure to be with people so full of enthusiasm for a place they loved.

We walked through the front doors and saw 1960s wall paneling everywhere. The years of remodeling had changed the building for both good and bad—good being air-conditioning, a new elevator, a renovated auditorium. On the other hand, Fred and Dale both mourned the removal of a grand entrance stairway and the old woodwork. "If we only had 50 million dollars," Dale said wistfully.

When the door of the elevator opened at the upper level, we entered a small well-lit room. To our right was a set of double doors, behind which was the attic. Just a few more steps, and we suddenly found ourselves in another world. It was a huge, empty, vaulted space of adz-hewn beams, darkened with age, and exposed handmade brick walls. Dominating the very center of the space, was a spiral staircase gracefully circling its way up to a rooftop cupola.

This was a wooden masterpiece of 19th-century engineering and joinery, and we could really sense the craftsmen's pride. "I believe it's the tallest free-standing spiral stairway in the state," Fred explained. As John began shooting, Dale asked "Do you want to climb up to the cupola? The view is amazing." John's only phobia has to do with heights, which Dale thought a bit ironic, for someone doing a book called *2nd Stories*. But it certainly looked inviting so, following Dale's lead, John started climbing. However, half way up, his rational mind couldn't conquer his increasing vertigo, and he turned and headed back down. For us, the inside view was amazing enough. —LB

Cupola (Merom Conference Center), Merom—Sullivan Co. (496-12)

Attic stair (Merom Conference Center), Merom—Sullivan Co. (581-10)

Large-scale model airplanes and helicopter—Warrick Co. (513-04)

Railroad crossing signal, Seymour—Jackson Co. (542-10)

Colgate-Palmolive Co., Clarksville—Clark Co. (569-10)

Greyhound Bus Terminal, Evansville—Vanderburgh Co. (558-07)

Building detail, Richmond—Wayne Co. (502-08)

Building detail, Huntingburg—Dubois Co. (552-02)

Building detail, Batesville—Ripley Co. (500-10)

Building detail, Boonville—Warrick Co. (566-08)

Building detail (Otis Park Clubhouse), Bedford—Lawrence Co. (505-15)

Building detail, Cambridge City—Wayne Co. (502-04)

Skylight (former bank), Greensburg—Decatur Co. (525-03)

Courthouse rotunda, Brazil—Clay Co. (488-07)

Ballroom (Knights of Pythias Building), Shelbyville—Shelby Co. (523-06)

Knights of the Pythias Lodge

"That tall building really looks like it could be interesting on the inside." John had repeated this phrase often over the past several months, as we scouted Indiana's downtowns for good shots. Here, in Shelbyville, he'd already photographed the exteriors of a number of old storefronts. We particularly liked a Victorian façade announcing in bold letters that it was a local jeweler (page 105). Now, crossing the street and exploring the other side of the Square, John was looking up at a possible treasure—a grand, but vacant, Lodge building (back cover). But how could we get in?

After asking several people on the street if they knew who owned the place, we learned that George Lux was the man to see—and he could be found just around the corner at Lux Realty. But the office manager said George was out of town. Then she added that his son, Larry, might be able to help. He was an officer at the Shelby County Bank—again, only a few doors away. A receptionist rang his office and we were soon face-to-face with Larry Lux in the bank's lobby. Although he was busy, once we explained our mission, he was eager to give us a tour of the old building. As the three of us walked over together, Larry took care of some business on his cell phone.

As he unlocked the door, our guide explained that, for many years, the first floor had been occupied by Murphy's Dime Store then, later, it was home to an antique store. Now, the entire building was vacant. Larry said his dad owned a number of downtown buildings and, because there didn't seem to be a rental market for the upstairs space, he hadn't been very enthusiastic about fixing up, or renting, the upper floors. As a result, nothing had been done to them for decades. Realizing that we were entering a time capsule of sorts, we climbed a substantial wooden stairway to the

Stair (K–P Building), Shelbyville—Shelby Co. (523-15)

Office (K–P Building), Shelbyville—Shelby Co. (523-03)

second floor. Larry said these upper levels had been home to various small offices, as well as the Knights of the Pythias Lodge.

Despite the dull, discolored walls, the dust, and the stale air, it was apparent that Larry Lux had a real fondness for the place. He appreciated the boulevard-wide hallways, tall ceilings, wood-and-glass-partitioned offices, even the small kitchen—but especially the once majestic Lodge Ballroom. Of course, he also realized how the heating, cooling, plumbing, and electrical systems needed to be brought up-to-date, and how the place needed elevators, modern restrooms, and insulation. In other words, before this marvelous space could really be used again, it would require the works. "But," Larry said hopefully, "it might be possible some day." We guessed that he had dreamed about a glorious restoration more than once.

However, even if it was fixed up, who would rent it, and for what purpose? It was sad to think it might just continue to languish, but what other choice was there? He wondered. We wondered. Then his cell phone rang for the third time, and he had to leave—but we could stick around to finish our photography. "Just be sure to lock the door," he said, "I'll come back later to turn out the lights."

After admiring, and shooting, John and I grew more and more mesmerized by the faded beauty around us. This building had once been a source of pride, a place of business, fraternity, and happy times. Now, it was a reminder of how one era's opulence is fleeting—how an extravagant, massive, once busy building can become passé. —LB

Iron stairway, Scottsburg—Scott Co. (576-09)

Iron stairway, North Vernon—Jennings Co. (573-06)

Painted store sign, Bedford—Lawrence Co. (466-03)

Painted store sign, Rising Sun—Ohio Co. (521-14)

Painted store sign, Edwardsport—Knox Co. (548-14)

Attic (Courthouse), Greenfield—Hancock Co. (507-13)

Coca-Cola® building, Tell City—Perry Co. (539-10)

Front desk (French Lick Springs Resort), French Lick—Orange Co. (577-15)

Building detail (Town Hall), Cynthiana—Posey Co. (513-08)

Upstairs (New Amsterdam General Store), New Amsterdam—Harrison Co. (563-03)

Stairway (Cloverdale Hardware Store), Cloverdale—Putnam Co. (491-09)

(Above) Founded in 1887, the Cloverdale Hardware Store is the oldest continuously operating hardware store in Indiana. Because the second floor is off-limits to the public, the stairway has become a display area.

(Left) The New Amsterdam General Store's upper level was once the meeting room for the local chapter of the International Order of Odd Fellows, and lodge symbols are still visible on the wallpaper. Today, this space is home to several large floor looms, as well as a selection of weaving and craft supplies. The building was erected in 1886.

Attic (Working Men's Institute), New Harmony—Posey Co. (580-14)

Attic (Working Men's Institute), New Harmony—Posey Co. (580-10)

Working Men's Institute

It was a hot July afternoon when we crossed the threshold of New Harmony's Working Men's Institute (WMI). We had made an appointment several days earlier, so Manager Frank Smith was expecting us, and greeted us by name as we lumbered in with our photography gear. The Board of Directors had given John and I permission to visit the attic, and had told Frank that he'd need to accompany us. But, with it being a tourist-season weekend, he'd also need to be available to other visitors. As the only staff person on duty, he apologized about having to divide his attention as circumstances dictated.

During a lull, when he could safely focus on us, Frank led us up the rarely used steps leading to the attic. Following closely behind, John and I grew increasingly eager to discover what hidden treasures awaited. This old and most noble institution just had to have neat stuff—all stored out of sight—up here, under the rafters.

Founded in 1838, with a generous endowment by William Maclure (a wealthy factory-owner and a member of Robert Owen's utopian experiment), the Working Men's Institute has always had a singular purpose—"the diffusion of useful knowledge" to the laboring classes. Maclure was so dedicated to this end that, eventually, 144 other WMIs were established throughout the state—but this was the only one left.

Today, the New Harmony Working Men's Institute is housed in an 1894 Romanesque brick structure with a requisite tower. It contains the oldest continuously operating library in the state. The first floor contains a wing for modern books, and a separate wing for historic volumes and archives. Half of the second floor is home to a marvelous natural

Attic (Working Men's Institute), New Harmony—Posey Co. (580-15)

Attic (Working Men's Institute), New Harmony—Posey Co. (580-11)

history museum straight out of the 19th century, and a waterway transportation display, complete with professionally produced audiovisuals. Of course, all this was quite interesting, and we had scrutinized it in some depth on previous visits. But on this day, we were here to see an area that's usually inaccessible.

As Frank unlocked the garret door, we followed closely behind, holding our breath. Then, as we passed through the doorway, I let out a squeal of delight and John gasped. It was absolutely wonderful! John said it was just how he imagined a museum's attic should be.

There was a cabinet covered in stone and plaster heads, some, perhaps, of once notable community leaders. There were handmade spinning wheels, aged dental equipment, taxidermied beasts and birds, cases of ancient books, old chairs, antique musical instruments, globes, old farming tools. All was softly illuminated by the dim light filtering through small gable windows, and a few bare incandescent bulbs. "Take photographs of whatever you like, but watch out for the spiders," Frank warned.

Undaunted, but alert for spiders, John took photo after photo. Then, hearing the ringing of a brass bell on the front door (which indicated someone was entering the building), we gathered our gear, and headed back downstairs. Frank locked the attic door and, with quick steps, made his way to the foyer to see who had arrived. As we reentered the high-ceilinged lobby, John put his gear away and we thanked our host. How grateful we were for this special excursion into the Institute's hidden upper storerooms. —LB

Hydraulic elevator mechanism (Fosdick Interiors), Liberty—Union Co. (503-07)

Abandoned factory (Golden Castings), Columbus—Bartholomew Co. (543-02)

Railroad bridge (Wabash River), Riverton—Sullivan Co. (497-03)

Former railroad bridge (Wabash River)—Knox Co. (529-03)

Each of these Wabash River railroad bridges was originally constructed as a "swing bridge" with the center span mounted on a giant turntable atop a circular limestone pier. This allowed the span to rotate out of the way, permitting riverboats to pass. The bridges no longer rotate, and the one above (which once carried the Wabash Cannonball) now carries single-lane automobile traffic.

Overhead passageway (Batesville Casket Co.), Batesville—Ripley Co. (500-13)

Overhead doors, Indianapolis—Marion Co. (564-12)

Alley stairway, Washington—Daviess Co. (548-03)

Fire escape (Masonic Lodge #580), Carthage—Rush Co. (508-13)

Fire escape (former high school), Pimento—Vigo Co. (476-08)

Clock (Farmers Mutual Insurance Co.), Brookville—Franklin Co. (518-11)

Clock (former Parker Jewelry), Seymour—Jackson Co. (542-04)

Attic (Courthouse), Bloomington—Monroe Co. (482-05)

Monroe County Courthouse

Inside the Monroe County Commissioners office, a smiling Jane Marie Lind greeted us with a friendly hello. The County Attorney had prepared two liability-release forms, and she had them ready for us to sign. After affixing our signatures, it was official—if we were maimed or killed, we could not sue, and the county wouldn't be liable. Of course, having photographed scores of dilapidated houses, collapsing barns, abandoned stores, and deteriorating factories, the innards of a Courthouse dome didn't seem like much of a risk to us.

Moments later, Jerry Appleberry arrived. As head of Security and Maintenance, he led us through an out-of-the-way doorway and up a flight of stairs into a behind-the-scenes universe of exposed framing, plumbing lines, insulation, and electrical conduit. After ascending a final, steep stairway, we stood on a narrow, circular walkway that hugged the walls. We were above the stained-glass ceiling that hangs over the rotunda, yet below the arching roof—it felt as if we were mingling with the very viscera of the building.

I didn't know what to expect, but this certainly was wasn't it. The walls were made of brick and coarsely cut limestone, and there was a ramshackle booth suspended over the stained-glass-and-iron matrix of the ceiling below. Resembling an outhouse, this was the home of the clock mechanism. Four metal shafts emerged from it, each driving a clock face on the exterior of the outer dome. There was only a rough plank connecting the walkway we were standing on to the clock room. That anyone would ever choose to cross that board seemed preposterous.

Jerry assured us that he had, indeed, walked across into the clock room, as had a clock repairman. So, despite the precariousness of the aerial bridge before him, John felt that if others had made it, he could, too. With that, he bravely, but slowly, made his way across and into the booth with his camera and tripod. After defying Fate, he discovered the tiny space was too tight for a good shot of the mechanism, so he returned to the solidity of the walkway.

Attic stair (Courthouse), Bloomington—Monroe Co. (482-10)

Meanwhile, Jerry and I looked through the attic windows at the snow-covered surroundings. He pointed out the strings of holiday lights that he and his crew had recently draped around the Square. Jerry said when he first started working at the Courthouse, legions of pigeons lived inside the dome. After blocking their entry points, there had been inches of encrusted guano to remove—a job as hazardous as it was disgusting.

By now John was back on the main walkway, shooting the giant Courthouse bell. It was securely mounted to the structure of the building, and was activated by an electric solenoid. As John concentrated on taking shots from several angles, Jerry told me more about his work, his home, his family. Suddenly, GONG!

John and I both jumped. With hearts pounding wildly, it took us each a few seconds to realize what had happened. The great, cast-iron bell was simply doing its thing—mechanically indifferent to anyone standing next to it. When I looked over at Jerry, he was professionally cool and calm—and smiling. —LB

Crane (Indiana University construction site), Bloomington—Monroe Co. (478-14)

(Right) In Indiana's coal-mining territory, the top of an excavator can occasionally be seen, looming above a hill, off in the distance, but it can be difficult to determine its size. The operator of this massive piece of equipment sat approximately three stories off the ground. The bucket is large enough to hold a small automobile.

Abandoned coal excavator—Owen Co. (495-10)

Montgomery Feed Mill, Montgomery—Daviess Co. (549-05)

Williams Milling Co., Williams—Lawrence Co. (504-01)

Stairway—Spencer Co. (165-05)

59

Stairway—Owen Co. (227-05)

Alley stairway, Westport—Decatur Co. (499-11)

Stairway, Martinsville—Morgan Co. (489-14)

School stairway, Butlerville—Jennings Co. (519-15)

Building façade (former bank), Birdseye—Dubois Co. (550-01)

Building detail, Evansville—Vanderburgh Co. (559-08)

Building façade, Shelbyville—Shelby Co. (522-14)

Attic window (Benjamin Franklin School), Tell City—Perry Co. (486-14)

Attic (Courthouse), Greenfield—Hancock Co. (508-02)

Interior of dome (Monastery Immaculate Conception), Ferdinand—Dubois Co. (555-13)

Monastery Immaculate Conception

We followed the Garden Tour signs to a lengthy set of steps and a long access ramp. Both led to the imposing buildings of the Monastery Immaculate Conception. I chose the concrete incline because it looked less demanding, and John went up the steps.

Even from a great distance, these brick structures dominated the landscape. But up close, they were even more impressive, especially the high-domed church. No wonder the Monastery's literature refers to it as "the castle on the hill." It was truly breathtaking.

We went through a side entry door and were greeted by two smiling nuns. "Are you here for the garden tour?" the older one asked. "Actually, we would like to photograph the interior of the church, if that's possible," John politely responded.

Immediately, a delighted Sister Carlita Koch volunteered to show us around. We followed as she opened a heavy door leading into the church. "It's being remodeled and restored, and I don't know how to turn the lights on. Another nun knows more about all this, but she's not around right now."

The lack of lights didn't matter. Even in the dim light, it was obvious we were in a rare and wonderful place. The walls had a fresh coat of light-green paint and there was gold gilt highlighting the raised decorations. A

Monastery Immaculate Conception, Ferdinand —Dubois Co. (553-05)

new white-and-caramel marble floor was nearing completion. Up above, ten tall angels with folded wings encircled the front. Two more looked down beatifically from the rear.

Sister Carlita described the work that had already been done. She also said the pews were due to arrive soon, and there would be a brand new altar, positioned "so the action and drama are closer to the people."

Construction for this magnificent church began in 1915, and was finished in 1924 (work had been halted for a few years due to WWI). And, now, the church was being totally rejuvenated and updated. It would have "a feminine feel to it," Sister Carlita smiled, saying a female designer had been consulted so the interior would better reflect a building used almost exclusively by women. Already considered an architectural treasure (it's on the National Register of Historic Places), we could tell that, when the restoration was finished, the church would be even more beautiful than before.

As we guessed, this extensive overhaul was very costly. To pay for it, the sisters have solicited funds from many people interested in preserving the monastery, and the work has had to be scheduled into two phases. Phase I (the outside) had already been completed and Phase II (the inside) was now in its final stages.

John set up his camera directly below the center of the arching dome and snapped away. After he was finished, Sister Carlita suggested we visit the adjoining reception area. It had an amazingly detailed miniature model of the entire Monastery. We learned how the original sisters stationed here were French, but the German-speaking Sisters of St. Benedict had been summoned from Kentucky to replace them. It seems they were a better fit with the area's German/Swiss population. At one time, there were 500 nuns in residence, but today there are only 126, many of whom are retired.

As John put his camera way, we learned that it might be possible to go up into the dome itself to photograph the sanctuary from up above. However, with so much construction still under way, that would have to wait for another day. —LB

Entry (Monastery), Ferdinand—Dubois Co. (553-12)

Tower (Monastery), Ferdinand—Dubois Co. (553-10)

Sculptural detail (VFW Post #1405), Spencer—Owen Co. (494-03)

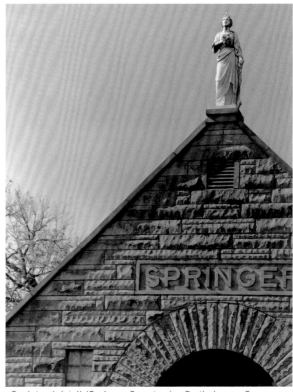

Sculptural detail (Springer Cemetery)—Bartholomew Co. (542-13)

Sculptural detail (Carnegie Center), New Albany—Floyd Co. (568-11)

Sculptural detail (St. Mary's), Greensburg—Decatur Co. (579-09)

Sculptural detail (St. Joseph Catholic Church), Jasper—Dubois Co. (551-06)

Building detail (former Cannelton Mill), Cannelton—Perry Co. (539-06)

Ruins (Washington Township Public School), Raleigh—Rush Co. (510-06)

Donner Hall (Hanover College), Hanover—Jefferson Co. (575-11)

Frady Methodist Church, Raglesville—Daviess Co. (535-03)

Former Courthouse, Rome—Perry Co. (485-03)

Waverly United Methodist Church, Waverly—Morgan Co. (477-15)

Former Town Hall/Fire Engine House, Huntingburg—Dubois Co. (551-14)

Building detail, Greensburg—Decatur Co. (524-12)

Building detail, Bloomfield—Greene Co. (533-15)

Building façade, Linton—Greene Co. (526-08)

Building detail, Petersburg—Pike Co. (532-04)

Building detail (Dr. Pirtle building), Carlisle—Sullivan Co. (497-06)

Dr. Pirtle's Surgery

As John started setting up his tripod and camera, I began to enter data about the shot into our Apple laptop. For this particular frame, I was able to type in all the pertinent information, except the address. "Main Street," I thought to myself, "It's probably Main Street." But, just to be sure, I got out of the car, walked to the corner, and looked up, only to discover there weren't any street signs. Just then, I spotted a lone tattooed man, dressed in worn jeans and sleeveless sweatshirt walking a rambunctious German shepherd. The pair had just emerged from an alley and were headed down the sidewalk. For some reason, despite his biker-like appearance, and his big dog, I wasn't at all intimidated. I just knew he'd know the name of the street. And, he did—Ledgerwood. "Ledgerwood?" I repeated.

He kindly explained that Carlisle was one of the few Indiana towns whose main street wasn't Main Street—it was named instead for a city father. With that settled, he smiled and asked what we were up to. When I said we were intrigued by the "Dr. Pirtle" on the top of the building, he became exuberant. Why, he knew all about the good doctor. When John strolled over, he told us how, in the early days of the town, it had been handy having Dr. Pirtle across the street from the saloon. That way, when someone got shot or stabbed in a bar brawl (apparently a common occurrence), it was a simple matter to carry the victim across the street and up the stairs to the surgery. He then added the fact that there was still a small operating room upstairs, complete with an overhead skylight.

Thus began our acquaintance with Doughboy. Originally from Connecticut, he had, indeed, been a member of a motorcycle club. He was also a disabled veteran (Airborne), and was an accomplished chef. And he lived on the first floor of Dr. Pirtle's building. His apartment had once been a motorcycle shop, which is what drew him to Carlisle. When the business folded and the space was converted into a residence, he promptly moved in with his dog, Sigmund.

Surgery (Dr. Pirtle building), Carlisle—Sullivan Co. (529-05)

Apartment (Dr. Pirtle building), Carlisle—Sullivan Co. (529-11)

Doughboy (a name bestowed on him by his brother when they were kids) said he liked living in Indiana, because "it had more room to move around in" than New England. He seemed very pleased with his adopted town, which was a good thing because he was somewhat stranded, having lost both his driver's license and wheels when he crashed his Harley into the rear of a police car.

Doughboy really wanted to show us the old 2nd-floor surgery, which he said had been converted into an apartment, but was now empty. So, we waited as he phoned his landlady to ask if she could bring over the key. Unfortunately, she was too busy at the moment, but Doughboy assured us he would get the key—if we could come back another day. We agreed and, a few weeks later, we returned to Carlisle.

When we spotted Doughboy, he was eager to give us "the tour." The entry door was already unlocked, so we headed up the narrow wooden steps. The second floor was dingy and cluttered with debris, yet, to our surprise and delight, Dr. Pirtle's surgery was still intact with its original skylight, just as Doughboy had described. Along with its unusual overhead light source, the tiny room had two doors and three large glass transoms opening into adjacent rooms. It was unlike any room we'd ever seen. We speculated that the transoms were for cross ventilation, or to allow natural sunlight from the skylight to illuminate the rest of the office. As I began looking around, John started shooting—as did Doughboy, with his digital camera. He seemed to have a passion for photographing dilapidated objects that had a local history. Having earlier looked at some photos of Sigmund, we could tell he had a good eye for composition.

As we started down the steps, Doughboy invited us for dinner. He'd made lasagna and had plenty. It sounded tempting, but John and I were running late. After saying good-bye, we got in our car and headed off, down Ledgerwood. —LB

Building detail, Orleans—Orange Co. (505-08)

Building façade (Evansville St. Hospital)—Vanderburgh Co. (560-10)

Building detail, Birdseye—Dubois Co. (550-06)

Building façade, Sullivan—Sullivan Co. (527-08)

Building façade, Millhousen—Decatur Co. (500-06)

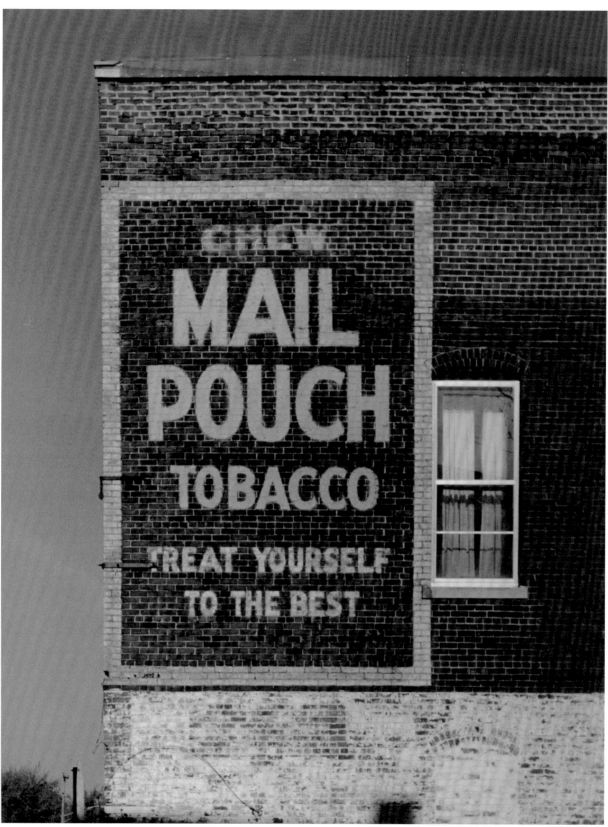

Painted wall advertisement, Lyons—Greene Co. (530-02)

Painted wall advertisement, Edwardsport—Knox Co. (548-11)

Round barn interior—Dearborn Co. (521-04)

Round barn interior—Rush Co. (509-02)

(Left) This round barn was originally a dairy barn, but now houses a Mack truck dealership. Although all the rafters are mysteriously bowed sideways, it is still structurally sound. With a height of 100' and a diameter of 100', it is one of the largest round barns in Indiana.

Windmill—Morgan Co. (490-12)

Barn detail—Martin Co. (535-06)

Barn roof with advertising—Orange Co. (556-05)

When Americans first took to the roads in the first half of the 20th century, barn roofs were popular, and convenient, billboards—particularly for tourist destinations. With the construction of the Interstate Highway System, long-distance traffic patterns changed radically, resulting in fewer examples like these remaining.

Barn roof with advertising—Martin Co. (546-12)

The Hay Press

As our car idled next to the rustic gatehouse of O'Bannon Woods State Park, we wondered if our trip might be unrewarded—again. When we'd visited a few weeks earlier, we'd forgotten about the time-zone difference and had arrived after closing. Today, even though it was just before lunch, we decided to ask the gate attendant if he could check and see if someone was manning the Nature Center. He smiled, and said "No problem." After a brief exchange on the phone, he said "Yes, somebody is definitely there. I'm sorry to say that the hay press won't be in operation though, but you can sure take pictures of it. Good luck." For a still photographer like John, no movement was a plus, so we drove on through.

Within minutes we were walking past the Pioneer Prairie Garden, approaching a large reconstructed timber-frame-and-pegged barn. As I stopped to admire the dark-pink cone flowers, John headed toward the nearby Nature Center, where he knew there would be someone who could let us into the loft so he could photograph the main workings of the 3-story hay press.

Hay Press, O'Bannon Woods State Park—Harrison Co. (577-07)

Once inside the attractive modern structure, he found part-time DNR Interpreter, Carla Striegel, on duty. John had met Carla, and Richard Langdon, a couple of years earlier through the Sun Oak Trading Post, which they operate in the town of English. They sell regional handmade art and crafts—as well as our Studio Indiana books. After sharing mutual greetings, they strolled back to the barn.

With a whoosh, Carla unlocked, and swung open, the barn doors at the top of an earthen ramp. She explained how this 1850s hay press was one of only about 12 left in the country, and it was the only one that had been restored. She said there used to be hundreds of them dotting the Ohio River Valley. Most were located in Ohio and Indiana, where a combination of good soil and temperate climate was ideal for growing hay. This was an important business because, prior to the age of automobiles, hay was an indispensable fuel for hungry horses in America.

Using the press was a relatively simple procedure. Local farmers brought in loose hay and forked it into a rectangular box. Then, with the help of a draft animal, a heavy wooden block (weighing 800–1,000 pounds) was forced down onto the hay, compacting it into a compressed bale. Once tied with twine, it was transported by boat or barge to markets such as Louisville. Though primitive by today's standards, this device was state-of-the-art in its day.

As John photographed the handmade machine, I strolled out back and became acquainted with Lion, a magnificent chestnut ox who was harnessed to the hay press during public demonstrations. Decoratively adorned with protective brass balls on his horn tips, he was aloof and proud. He contrasted, in every respect, with his corral mates—a pair of gregarious gray-brown donkeys.

All too quickly, John was done shooting. With his equipment packed up, we said farewell to the animals and Carla. It had certainly been worth the return visit. —LB

Hay Press, O'Bannon Woods State Park—Harrison Co. (577-10)

Former factory (third floor), Indianapolis—Marion Co. (516-08)

Industrial chimney, Indianapolis—Marion Co. (056-14)

Tulip Trestle—Greene Co. (533-11)

Abandoned railroad bridge (Ohio River), Jeffersonville—Clark Co. (570-12)

(Left) At 2,307 feet, the Tulip Trestle is the third longest bridge of its type in the world. Also known as the Greene Co. Viaduct, it was built in 1906 and stands 157 feet off the ground at its highest point. The construction was such a massive and unique undertaking, families would have picnic dinners in the area to watch the bridge being built.

Window view (Buskirk-Chumley Theater office), Bloomington—Monroe Co. (478-07)

Kirkwood Hall (Indiana University), Bloomington—Monroe Co. (479-09)

Building façade, Bloomfield—Greene Co. (534-02)

Building façade, Lawrenceport—Dearborn Co. (521-11)

Building façade, Salem—Washington Co. (557-09)

Building façade, Columbus—Bartholomew Co. (545-08)

Building façade (former Second National Bank), Vincennes—Knox Co. (527-12)

Building façade, North Vernon—Jennings Co. (572-05)

Building façade, Boonville—Warrick Co. (566-04)

Building detail, Madison—Jefferson Co. (574-11)

Sculptural detail (Chanticleer Building), Terre Haute—Vigo Co. (475-10)

Old Morgan County Jail

It was a brisk March day when we walked into Jailbird Antiques. Aptly named, the shop occupies part of an 1890, red-brick, 2-story, Italianate jailhouse. Before being retired, the building housed both prisoners and turnkey in the Morgan County seat of Martinsville. Inside, we were greeted by a buoyant Tina Chafey, one of the two proprietresses (the other being Judy Krick). Tina had suggested we stop by at two o'clock when activity in the Tea Room typically slowed down. Looking around, I saw hummingbird trinkets, books, antique clothing, and more—the first floor didn't even hint at its former use. Because the customers had not thinned out as expected, Tina told us to go on upstairs, that she would be with us in a few minutes.

To pass the time, we explored several cells that were filled with an odd assortment of items for sale—treasures such as a handmade acrylic baboon, Edwardian-era women's shoes, and a 1967 high-school yearbook. Two of the rooms, also former cells, had doors constructed of iron straps in a crisscross pattern that were perfect for displaying pictures and vintage dresses. "Squad Room" was painted in flaking gold letters on a glass transom leading to an old office.

Former jail, Martinsville—Morgan Co. (499-02)

After a short time, Tina brought a key to unlock the heavy steel door leading into the main cellblock. There was no electricity, and we had to watch out for the 10" holes in the floor. However, our eyes soon adjusted to the only light available, which was filtering through the glass pane of an outer door. I peered out, and realized that the door opened into 2 stories of thin air. Meanwhile, Tina was pointing out some interesting graffiti and a skull drawn by a prisoner. The paint everywhere was peeling, but Tina assured us that it had been tested and, while unattractive, it was completely lead-free.

As we wandered from cell to cell, Tina told us how a parapsychology group had recently been by. They claimed to have sensed the presence of a dead man. Tina found this information quite unsettling, and didn't like the idea of a specter living in her place of daily employment. John and I couldn't sense any departed souls (and none showed up on film). Perhaps whoever he was, he was now gone—or maybe he was visiting the "Garden Room" down on the first floor, admiring the decorative flower stakes and tinkling wind chimes for a more pleasant change of scenery.

Despite very limited light and cramped maneuvering space, John managed to set up his camera and tripod and start shooting. Because it was so dark, he needed to take exceptionally long exposures—as much as a full minute—but he was unable to see his watch to time them. That's when he handed me his trusty digital Timex. I stood in the sorry light provided by the door-to-nowhere and, squinting, called out "Time" for the end of each shot.

Before leaving, as we gathered our gear, we glanced around one last time. Such a primitive place—bleak, colorless, depressing, and comfortless—it was difficult to believe these dismal cells were still in use as recently as 1991. It was this unsettling fact, not ghosts, that haunted me. —LB

Former jail, Martinsville—Morgan Co. (498-15)

"City of Mineral Water" sign (rear view), Martinsville—Morgan Co. (489-09)

K-P sign (Knights of Pythias), Bloomington—Monroe Co. (478-12)

Building façade, Salem—Washington Co. (557-02)

Building detail (Clothing Hall), Vincennes—Knox Co. (527-14)

Building façade, Vincennes—Knox Co. (527-15)

Building façade (City Hall), Seymour—Jackson Co. (567-13)

Building detail (former Sheldon Jewelers), Shelbyville —Shelby Co. (522-09)

Steeple restoration (St. Boniface Catholic Church), Fulda—Spencer Co. (539-01)

Steeple restoration (St. George Lutheran Church)—Shelby Co. (507-08)

Former Methodist-Episcopal Church, Vandalia—Owen Co. (488-12)

First Christian Church, Greensburg—Decatur Co. (525-14)

Fire Station No. 1, Lawrenceburg—Dearborn Co. (521-08)

Springfield Methodist Church—Franklin Co. (503-08)

Tyson Temple United Methodist Church, Versailles—Ripley Co. (574-03)

Shelter roof (Garfield Park), Indianapolis—Marion Co. (564-06)

Upper-level porch (French Lick Springs Resort), French Lick—Orange Co. (578-10)

Bedford Masonic Lodge

Moses Dunn's name is familiar to many in Lawrence County. For example, the local hospital is named for him. However, there is a legacy that's less well known—Masonic Lodge #14, which sits on the courthouse square. While Europe was engaged in The Great War (WWI), Dunn donated a 2-story building that housed his law office, and $50,000 cash, to construct a new Masonic Lodge. With these generous gifts as inspiration, fellow Masons raised an additional $60,000, tore down the law building, bought the adjacent lot, hired an architect, and built the impressive, multi-storied, limestone structure that graces the downtown to this day. Despite a cornerstone date of 1917, it has a strikingly modern façade, with neoclassic overtones.

Stan Ritchison, Past Master of the Blue Lodge, unlocked the doors for us, eager to show us around, proud of the Lodge's history, proud of Masonry, and proud of his Lodge brothers. He had personally cleaned and painted several rooms and organized various displays. He had also updated the record-keeping methods, and had been instrumental in getting energy-efficient replacement windows, a new roof, and a 14-furnace heating system installed.

There was so much to explore—from a small game room, to tiny closets, to spacious lodge quarters with high ceilings and balconies—and Ritchison showed us them all. The main Blue Lodge room, where his order met, was most impressive. There were throne-like seats, and tall walls painted a vibrant salmon, cream, and azure blue. A mysterious stairway rising up to a short mezzanine against the back wall caught my eye. Ritchison said it was used for certain teaching/initiation rites and there were only a handful of such symbolic structures left in Indiana lodges.

On a higher floor, was a space used by the York Order. With heavy velvet curtains hanging behind a series of arches on each side, this grand space also had throne-like seats. Most intriguing was a narrow dressing room with metal lock-

View (Masonic Lodge), Bedfford—Lawrence Co. (512-01)

Ventilating fan (Masonic Lodge), Bedford—Lawrence Co. (512-10)

ers, forlorn trunks, and forgotten suitcases. Inside, were a few ostrich-plumed black hats, reminiscent of the headgear worn by the captain of the HMS Pinafore. On wire coat hangers, inside lockers and closets, we could see old dress uniforms and sashes—now covered with dust.

As Ritchison picked up a disintegrating hat, he said that many of these marvelous accouterments had been left behind, as members died, became incapacitated, or moved away. Because the York Order hadn't required members to wear elaborate outfits for some time, the dressing room had been retired years ago. John and I felt like Howard Carter entering King Tut's tomb, and I was reminded of my father, a 32nd-degree Mason in Detroit, who had worn one of these outfits and enjoyed the camaraderie of his fellow members. When I was a child, he told me how his Lodge building had been specifically designed to withstand the thundering vibration of the men marching in unison.

The uppermost level of the Lodge building housed a prestigious ballroom. With huge glass windows overlooking the Courthouse, it had been a spectacular space but, now, was unused, dingy, and rundown. Stan said there was a glass wall behind some recently installed plywood, with doors opening onto the roof for guests to enjoy outdoor dancing or a bit of fresh air. The high cost of heating had necessitated the plywood barrier—but the original structure had been saved for possible reuse in the future.

Almost as an afterthought, Stan opened a closet door adjacent to the elevator. Inside was a giant "60" Universal Blower" which had once been the lungs of the original air-handling system. Quite a marvel in ventilation for its day, it was no longer in use but, always impressed by mechanical devices, John took several photographs of it. And, with that, what we had assumed would be a 20-minute tour, was over—after an hour and a half. —LB

Storage room (Masonic Lodge), Bedford—Lawrence Co. (512-07)

Porch-roof observatory, Elizabeth—Harrison Co. (562-15)

Goethe Link Observatory (owned by Indiana University)—Morgan Co. (353-10)

Microwave tower, Terre haute—Vigo Co. (474-06)

High-voltage power-line towers—Spencer Co. (566-15)

Derrick (abandoned limestone quarry)—Monroe Co. (468-12)

Conveyer (Haydite manufacturing plant)—Morgan Co. (498-06)

Conveyers (coal distribution facility)—Knox Co. (548-08)

Wooden roller coaster (Holiday World), Santa Claus—Spencer Co. (567-08)

Covered aquaduct during restoration (Whitewater Canal State Historic Site), Metamora—Franklin Co. (517-06)

Barn roof detail—Rush Co. (510-07)

Abandoned schoolhouse, Philomath—Union Co. (502-13)

Soldiers' and Sailors' Children's Home

"Watch out for the carpet," warned Paul Wilkinson, Superintendent of the Indiana Soldiers' and Sailors' Children's Home. Underfoot, the garish floor covering was loose and rumpled. Draped haphazardly over the steps, it offered little in the way of security to anyone navigating the wide central stairway to the upper floors.

Built in 1867 by the Grand Army of the Republic as a sanctuary for children orphaned by the Civil War, this main building had been a majestic structure in its era—and it still was. Standing four-stories tall in a Victorian Italianate design, parts of its outer brick façade had been stuccoed to cover smoke damage from a disfiguring fire. Unable to meet modern building-and-safety codes due to the prohibitive costs involved, for the last 30 years all the upper floors have been closed off.

Originally, the Home's staff members, as well as throngs of young charges, lived in this building. Today, there are several attractive newer residences, a school, and other buildings in an academy-like setting with sweeping green lawns and a small lake. We were told that children between ages 3 and 18 are placed here for a variety of reasons. In some cases, their parents are in active military service, while others have parents who, for some reason, are temporarily unable to care for them. None of the children are legally available for adoption.

As we climbed the stairs, it became obvious that Paul loved his job—being in charge of one of the few state-run children's homes left in the U.S. With pride, he told us of the institution's current operation and its history. He explained how he and some of his staff were trying to organize and preserve old records that had long been neglected, so the heritage of the place would be there for future generations. As he spoke, his enthusiasm was both sincere and contagious.

Now we were traversing the last flight of steps. At the very top, Paul unlocked a door and we entered the vaulted attic space. The darkened wooden beams swept up impressively to a steeply pitched gable. Sunlight filtered in through windows on all sides. There were brick chimneys rising through the space, serving the many coal fireplaces that once provided heating. We gawked, walked, and looked around. It was an absolutely amazing space.

Despite being constructed nearly 140 years ago, the wood floor was surprisingly squeak-free, but I thought I heard an occasional chirping. Paul said they had successfully eliminated all the bats, but a few birds had found their way inside. Suddenly, I noticed tiny flashes of light high above. Several modern smoke detectors attached to the ceiling were announcing that they were on duty and fully functional. As it turned out, most of the attic was empty, but I did spot two large steel tubs with warped sides. They had once been used as cisterns, supplying water to the entire building. Two more were on the other side of the stairway entrance.

After John finished shooting, the three of us returned to the main floor. John asked Paul what his background was. Coincidentally, he had a degree in Industrial Education from Ball State University, as did John. Leaving the old building behind, we walked into the sunlight, and into a different time—our time. It actually took us several minutes to readjust to the 21st century and settle into our SUV. Like much in our contemporary world, our car was well crafted, comfortable, and reliable—but it couldn't compare to the magnificence and hand-craftsmanship of this massive old Childrens' Home we had just been privileged to visit. —LB

Frieze (Children's Home), Knightstown—Rush Co. (509-07)

Attic (Children's Home), Knightstown—Rush Co. (509-10)

Attic (Children's Home), Knightstown—Rush Co. (509-11)

Attic (Children's Home), Knightstown—Rush Co. (509-12)

Building detail, Vincennes—Knox Co. (528-04)

Building façade (Terminal Arcade), Terre Haute—Vigo Co. (487-14)

Sculptural detail, Evansville—Vanderburgh Co. (559-05)

Building façade (former bank), Rushville—Rush Co. (516-15)

Building detail (former bank), Vincennes—Knox Co. (528-03)

Building detail (former bank), Poseyville—Posey Co. (515-13)

129

Building detail, Columbus—Bartholomew Co. (468-14)

Building detail, Madison—Jefferson Co. (574-08)

Building detail, North Vernon—Jennings Co. (572-03)

Building detail, North Vernon—Jennings Co. (572-13)

Sculptural detail (Majestic Building), Indianapolis—Marion Co. (565-04)

Sculptural detail, Evansville—Vanderburgh Co. (559-06)

The Archabbey Church of Our Lady of Einsiedeln, St. Meinrad—Spencer Co. (538-09)

St. Meinrad Archabbey

We were on our way to meet Brother Maurus Zoeller in St. Anselem Hall. An impressive, old, institutional structure, it had been the monastery building before being remolding in the 1990s. Now a guest house, it was completely redone inside, with rooms and hallways bright and airy. After waiting briefly for our guide to arrive, we spotted a smiling, gentle looking monk coming our way. It was Brother Maurus.

"Are you ready for your tour?" He was obviously eager to begin. So, off we went. With Brother Maurus in the lead, we went outdoors, down through a manicured rock garden, and up into the church itself. As with most of St. Meinrad's structures, it was built of large blocks of caramel-colored sandstone, quarried nearby. Again, while the exterior projected an Old World feel, much of the interior had a more modern appearance.

This impressive structure—officially The Archabbey Church of Our Lady of Einsiedeln—once sat a thousand people. However, in recent years, it had been radically remodeled. For example, the balcony had been removed and the main floor was raised and covered with multi-hued marble. Downsized to fit current needs, it now seated about a hundred guests, retreatants, and students. Contrasting the otherwise minimalist feel, there were original stained-glass windows (imported from Germany), and a dark, heavy Presider's Chair.

Brother Maurus explained how St. Meinrad was one of only seven archabbeys in the world. Impressed, I asked him what Meinrad had done to earn sainthood. It seems he was a German hermit monk who, after being murdered, had developed a devoted following. I then kiddingly asked if they happened to have a saint's finger as a relic. To my surprise, we were ushered to a large bejeweled and golden structure. It contained the relics of several saints, and nearby was a small reliquary with a portion of the mortal remains of St. Meinrad himself.

Chapter Room (St. Meinrad Archabbey), St. Meinrad—Spencer Co. (537-08)

Because we knew Brother Maurus was busy, John assured him we could shoot pictures by ourselves if he wanted to return to work. With that, he showed us where the lights were, and wrapped up with a quick visit to the Oratory room and the Chapter Room. After thanking him for his guidance, we were now alone, scrutinizing a most interesting space.

 The Chapter Room had two rows of simple high-backed chairs, precisely positioned, facing each other, on either side of the long room. Light filtered through contemporary black-and-clear stained-glass windows—stunning and powerful in their stark simplicity. And there were murals everywhere. The ones on the ceiling were especially vivid and filled with an exuberant vitality. I particularly liked the panel depicting sea life, with writhing octopus tentacles and exotically colored fish. Surrounding them all, the signs of the twelve major constellations danced, while two larger-than-life, wooden-carved monks flanked the entry door with bowed heads.

After capturing several shots in the Chapter Room, we returned to photograph the church, where we met an electrician who had been up inside one of the steeples working on an antenna. Up there, he said, it was possible to see Tell City—almost 15 miles away. John had asked Brother Maurus earlier about going up into the towers, but was told they were off limits. No problem, there was plenty to shoot inside the church itself—the huge mural of the risen Christ, the lectern's nine bronze panels, the dramatically vaulted ceiling, the organ's 3,844 flamed-copper pipes.

After having finished off two rolls of film, and staying an hour longer than we'd originally planned, it was time to leave St. Meinrad. It had been a fascinating tour—the unexpected juxtaposition of Old World–New World, religious residents–lay guests, Romanesque stone towers–20th century interiors, formality–flamboyance, religious paintings–astrological symbols. Thank you, Brother Maurus for sharing your remarkable home with us. —LB

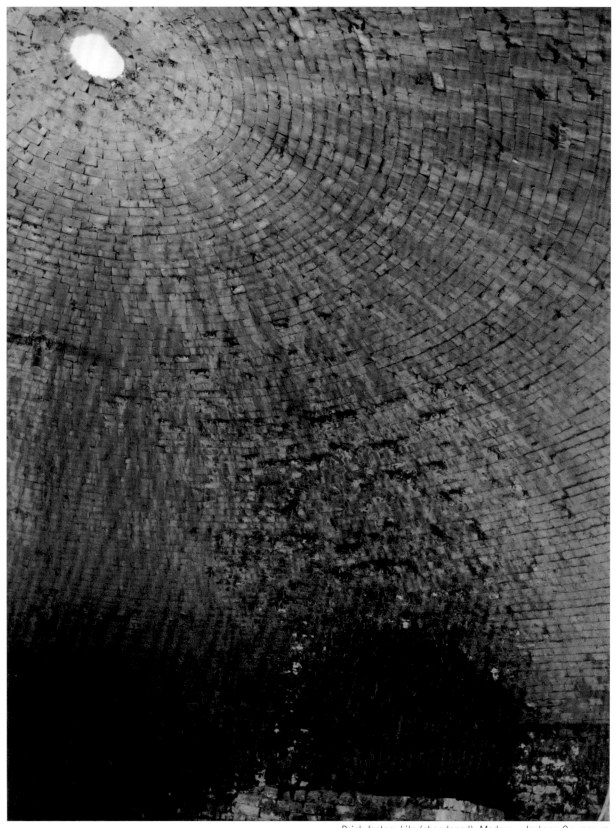

Brick-factory kiln (abandoned), Medora—Jackson Co. (541-13)

Lime-burning kiln (abandoned), Milltown—Crawford Co. (536-10)

Sign (Schmitt Furniture), New Albany—Floyd Co. (569-08)

Sign (Frigid Whip), Tell City—Perry Co. (486-12)

Sign (Mobile Manor), Columbus—Bartholomew Co. (471-01)

Sign (American Legion Post #124), Ferdinand—Dubois Co. (554-02)

Building detail (former bank), Huntingburg—Dubois Co. (552-10)

Building detail (former bank), Connersville—Fayette Co. (518-01)

Building façade (5/3 Bank), Poseyville—Posey Co. (580-03)

Marquee (Indiana Theater), Terre haute—Vigo Co. (474-10)

Building façade (Red Men's lodge), Franklin—Johnson Co. (480-14)

Building detail, Indianapolis—Marion Co. (564-11)

Building façade (former Pantheon Theater)—Knox Co. (528-11)

Sculptural detail (Courthouse), Princeton—Gibson Co. (532-02)

Afterword

When Lynn and I begin a book project like this, we start with a rough idea of where it will lead, but we don't even guess at what the final result will be. We've learned that, soon enough, our venture will take on a life of its own—urging us to go certain places, to include this, to omit that. We've both learned to trust, and dutifully follow, this intuitive process, because it always seems to be right.

When the idea for *2nd Stories* first emerged, we were already aware of interesting things up in the air. After all, being two people who enjoy looking around wherever we go, we had seen many of them. While we had no idea of the variety we would eventually come across, we just knew we'd find what we needed—and we did. For example, early on, we hadn't thought of including images of stairways. But as we started shooting, there they were—obviously important aspects of our journey. In the end, what makes a project like this so enjoyable is the evolution, the exploring, and the mysterious inevitability of it all.

Having become familiar with much of southern Indiana during explorations for our two previous photography books, we decided, once again, to limit our travels to that part of the state lying south of U.S. 40. Comprehensively covering all of Indiana would have simply been too big a project, and including images from all ninety-two counties would have shortchanged our subject. At first, we considered driving up and down every numbered highway in our chosen territory. But, as the project unfolded,

it seemed like it would be more revealing to go through each town marked on our map, many of which were on less-traveled side roads.

So that's we ending up doing. By driving 12,000 miles on a long series of day trips, we visited a total of 912 cities and towns—*every single one* shown on our official 2000 Indiana highway map. To help us find the out-of-the way places, we relied on an accordion folder filled with county maps. Still, we occasionally got lost, and had to depend on a compass to find our way to a recognizable landmark.

We roamed through cities and towns, large and small, ranging from major population centers (Indianapolis and Evansville) to tiny, nearly forgotten hamlets. While many of the communities retained their charm and vitality, others had vanished—a few so much so that there was absolutely nothing left, not even a stop sign.

Of course, we could have gotten plenty of pictures by limiting our search to county seats and bigger cities. But, if we had done that, we would have missed some real treasures in Indiana's smallest towns—such as the quaint schoolhouse in Philomath (page 121); Waverly's ethereal Methodist church (page 70); the deteriorating, yet noble, school tower in Raleigh (page 69); or the St. Boniface Church steeple in Fulda (page 106). Even though the majority of the places we visited didn't make the pages of this book, we are quite pleased to have passed through them, because these small towns are where much of Indiana's everyday history took place. Besides, it was a great deal of fun.

As is typical, we waited until midway through our project before approaching someone to write the Foreword. That's because it takes some time on the road, and in the darkroom, before a book starts to form a unique and cohesive identity. At first, we consider a wide range of possible candidates. Then, as images begin accumulating, and themes start materializing, we shorten our list to the most suitable contributors.

With *2nd Stories*, Lynn suggested Michael Atwood early in the process—as we watched him host "Across Indiana" on Public Television one evening. Because his name came up so quickly, we felt obliged to consider other possibilities, but no one seemed as appropriate. In short, Michael Atwood, with his long-time interest in all things Hoosier, and his insightful wit, was the perfect choice. After reading his Foreword, we're sure you'll agree. So, we'd like to take this opportunity to thank him for his kind and touching words.

We'd also like to express our gratitude to all the individuals who shared their time, stories, and special buildings with us. It was very refreshing to meet people with such a passion for their work and their surroundings. Finally, I'd like to offer a special thanks to the Indiana Arts Commission for awarding me an Individual Artist Grant to help in the publication of this book. —JB

Evening skyline, Oldenburg—Franklin County (519-02)